Woodchuckles

ISBN:1449503438

to order copies of this book, please visit

www.woodchuckles.com

Acknowledgements

Grateful thanks to Susan Spiro, Jaala Spiro, A. J. Hamler, Tod Riggio, Jim Harrold, Ken Brady, Ken Hahn, Ivan Troyer, Alvin Bontrager, Elizabeth Morrison, Corrina and Aden, Jacob Spiro, Kai and Zoe, and to the many trees I have used.

And thanks to every reader who laughs, grins, guffaws, giggles or grunts at these cartoons. Our laughter lights the world.

This book is dedicated:

To my dear love, Susan, who has cheerfully supported my fascination with creating wood furniture, knows a planer from a joiner and speaks loudly enough for me to hear;

To my ancestors, who did not know a mortise from a dovetail, and to my progeny who are proudly keeping that tradition alive;

To woodworkers everywhere—may your fingers be safe and nimble, your wallets full and your faces often laughing.

-- Steven Spiro

To Dad, who taught me life, love, laughter, and a lot about drawing.

-- Dave Sanders

Woodchuckles

Unable to afford a panel sander, Ned still saved
valuable time with his team of 80 grit shop cats.

Woodchuckles

Improvements in Snore Technology.

Woodchuckles

Woodchuckles

Medieval Furniture Repair

Woodchuckles

Yep...I reckon the Woodworkers are in town again.

Woodchuckles

Woodchuckles

Woodchuckles

Woodchuckles

Woodchuckles

Why fish quit woodworking.

Woodchuckles

Gurg Lorc attempts the first Mortise-and-Tenon and discovers fire instead.

Woodchuckles

Woodchuckles

Phil was glad he had his push stick with him.

Woodchuckles

Woodchuckles

Woodchuckles

Pinocchio as a young man.

Woodchuckles

When Glue Runs

Woodchuckles

Woodchuckles

The animals worked cheap, but the quality
just wasn't there.

Woodchuckles

Woodworkers describing a maple plank.

Woodchuckles

Irv never really got the hang of employee theft.

Woodchuckles

Woodchuckles

Fred never left home without his moisture meter.

Woodchuckles

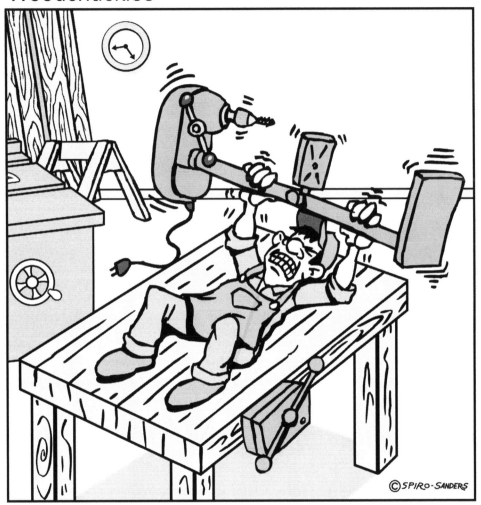

Since he couldn't afford the gym,
Ben worked out on the bench press.

Woodchuckles

Life among the Coarse Abrasives

Woodchuckles

X-treme Woodworking

Woodchuckles

A meeting in the board room.

Woodchuckles

Woodchuckles

Louise tries out her new "Stud Finder".

Woodchuckles

Before clamps.

Woodchuckles

At the Old Woodworkers' Home.

Woodchuckles

Dan loves his "dual-action" sander.

Woodchuckles

The Woodworker and his Lover

Woodchuckles

Early attempts at the table saw.

Woodchuckles

Woodchuckles

Fred figured he didn't really need a dust collection system.

Woodchuckles

Woodchuckles

Woodchuckles

Stan always felt paranoid when in possession of a joint.

Woodchuckles

Woodchuckles

Ray still used the old style fence for sentimental reasons.

Woodchuckles

Early attempts at the Planer.

Woodchuckles

Woodchuckles

Salvadore Dali in his basement woodshop.

Woodchuckles

Len was definitely aging.

Woodchuckles

Woodcutter Trog Velm inadvertently invents the catapult.

Woodchuckles

When Sawhorses Dream

Woodchuckles

Even the most warped boards responded to Ed.

Woodchuckles

Woodchuckles

Woodchuckles

Before tape measures.

Woodchuckles

Sven's wooden socks never caught on.

Woodchuckles

Woodchuckles

Woodchuckles

Early attempts at the Pneumatic Sander.

Woodchuckles

Just as Eskimos have many names for "snow",
woodworkers have a variety of terms for "dust".

Woodchuckles

Woodchuckles

Stan's dry kiln limited the size of his projects.

Woodchuckles

Woodchuckles

Jim knew size didn't really matter, but it bothered him anyway.

Woodchuckles

Woodchuckles

Woodchuckles

Woodchuckles

Woodchuckles

Another "bust" by the Hand Tool Police

Woodchuckles

Phil the Dentist enjoyed woodworking as a hobby.

Woodchuckles

Woodchuckles

Herb really didn't mind hand sanding.

Woodchuckles

Early attempts at the Circular Saw.

Woodchuckles

Woodchuckles

How much wood a Woodchuck can chuck.

Woodchuckles

When woodworkers go bad:
Counterfeiting wooden nickels.

Woodchuckles

Woodchuckles

When plumbers make furniture.

Woodchuckles

Pinocchio discovers the art of the cover-up

Woodchuckles

Woodchuckles

Woodchuckles

The Tape Measures visit their country cousins.

Woodchuckles

Woodchuckles

Though paternity was never established,
we do know the origin of sawhorses.

Woodchuckles

Mike just couldn't help admiring beautiful wood.

Woodchuckles

Irv's forth grade teacher often stopped by
to scold him for improper fractions.

Woodchuckles

Woodchuckles

Furniture repair in ancient China.

Woodchuckles

No matter how much "Endust" she used,
every night he came back.

Woodchuckles

Woodchuckles

Having experienced "kickback",
Clem revives the codpiece as a fashion statement.

Woodchuckles

Greg liked his antique tools,
but the apprentice was often ill-tempered.

Woodchuckles

Woodchuckles

Early attempts at kiln drying.

Woodchuckles

Woodchuckles

Woodchuckles

Woodchuckles

Furniture repair in the Old West

Woodchuckles

Woodchuckles

Woodchuckles

Stan's air dried Lumber always smelled so fresh!

Steven Spiro started out as a hippie toymaker in 1972. By 1976 he was a full-time professional furniture maker, a craft he still practices today. He always was a slow learner.

Now he has also become a mega-galactic cartoonist and the CEO of "Woodchuckles." When not woodworking or woodchuckling, he enjoys time with his family, grandchildren and friends in Wisconsin.

Steven's articles have been published in *Fine Woodworking* and *Fine Homebuilding* and his cartoons have appeared in *Woodshop News* and *Woodcraft* Magazine.

David W. Sanders has been drawing cartoons ever since he figured out which way to point a pencil. Many of his cartoons have been featured in various publications and he maintains a freelance business, Grinzday Graphic Design, in the Great Northwest.